Library of Congress Cataloguing Publication Data

ISBN Ebook: 979-8-9925557-3-8

ISBN Paperback: 979-8-9925557-2-1

Author: Emily Allen, MPA-Disaster Management Consultant
UNPREPARED, LLC

Cover design by: Fagraphy

Photography by: Emily Allen

Dedicated to my parents who guided me to be the person I am today.

Pastor/Superintendent J. B. Allen
Missionary Evelyn Allen

Inspired by my daughters:

Kimberly L. Allen
Alixyandra B. Allen

Message to My Daughters:

When faced with situations beyond your control,
decide how you will respond and see it as your chance to
transform adversity into resilience. Embrace the journey!

In Jesus Name, Amen!

CONTENTS

WHAT IF...?

Are you and your family PREPARED?

Introduction

      Disasters have been a part of human history since the beginning, striking communities around the globe, often some without warning and leaving lasting impacts. One of the oldest stories that highlights a disaster, and the importance of preparation is the story of Noah's Ark. When faced with a crisis, instincts drive us to seek safety for our loved ones, ensuring they are protected and secure, especially those who need extra support.

      Many people feel confident and believe they are ready to face a disaster like a hurricane, but the reality is often different. **'Hurricane Safety Measures'** is intended to empower young readers and their families with essential safety tips for hurricane preparedness, emphasizing steps to take before a storm, providing guidance on caring for pets, and offering strategies to reduce the impact of disasters. This information can make a difference in protecting one another during a crisis when it matters the most.

Preparing helps us stay safe and recover quickly!

WHAT YOU WILL LEARN

1. Basic hurricane safety measures.

2. Basic ways to help you be prepared and ready to take action.

3. Family evacuation plan.

4. Survival go-bags for the entire family (including your furry friends).

5. Ways to prepare for potential storms using a safety checklist

Working together to stay safe and prepared for the wild weather that Mother Nature brings our way is crucial to everyone!

Exploring Hurricanes

Hurricanes are powerful storms that form over the Atlantic and Pacific Oceans. When they approach land, they can bring heavy rain and strong winds that can be destructive to some communities. In different areas around the world, they may be called cyclones or typhoons.

While these storms can cause serious damage, like building collapses and disruptions to our daily lives, it's important to learn about them in order to stay safe. By understanding hurricanes and what they can do, young readers will have a knowledge-based approach and can feel more prepared with a know-how to assist their families when the time comes. It's all about everyone being informed, working together, and staying safe!

Effects of Hurricanes:

- Destructive to communities as homes and building are damaged or destroyed.

- Lights, water and gas stations are shut down.

- Power lines and trees are down

- Roads and transportation is limited or not drivable.

Hurricane Michael – 2018
(photograph by: Emily Allen)

NEVER shelter-in-place in a mobile home during a hurricane.

Hurricane Season – North America

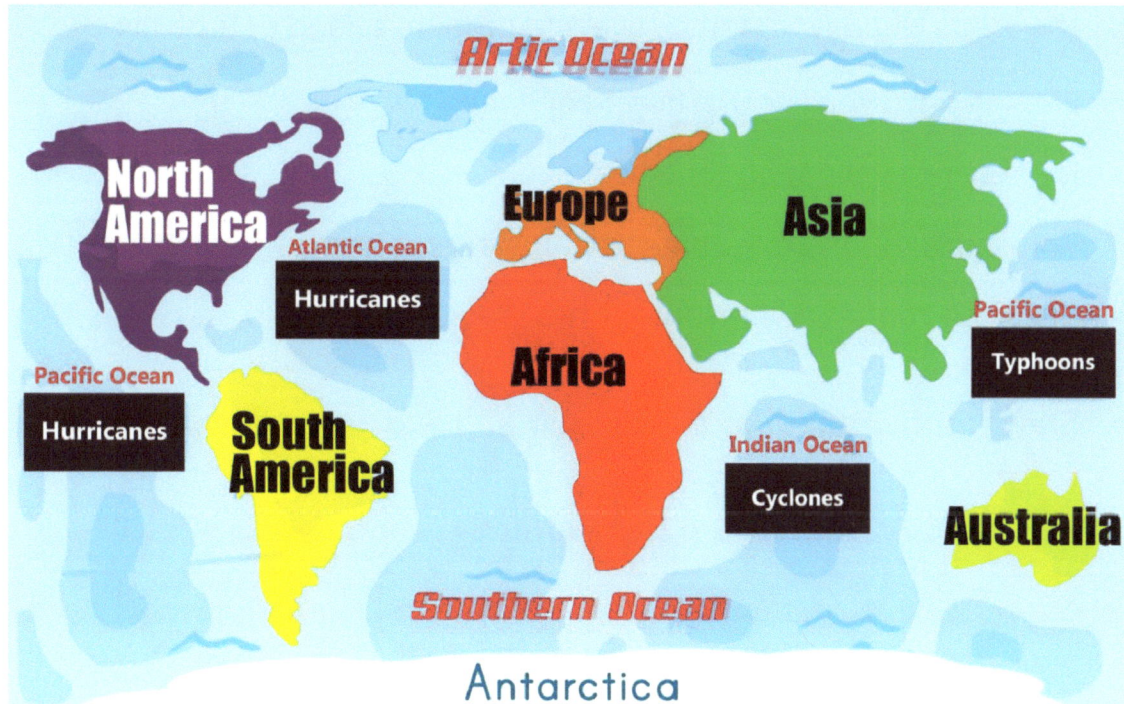

Atlantic Ocean: June – November

Pacific Ocean: May – November

Hurricane Season – North America (cont'd)

Know the areas where your family live and prepare ahead of time by:

- Finding out if you live in a flood-zone area.

- Identifying evacuation routes.

- Knowing if there are warning systems in your area

- Ensuring community resources are readily available if and when needed.

- Stay informed about your area's risk and response plans.

Preventions are more effective than the cure!

Hurricane Categories and Wind Speeds

Hurricanes are described in categories based on their wind speeds to help identify the strength of the storm. The higher the wind speed, the more damage they can cause to people, property and communities. Below are examples of hurricanes and their potential impact.

Number (Category)	Wind Speed (Miles Per Hour)	DAMAGE (Potential)	Storm Surge (Potential Height)
1	74-95	**Minimal:** affects unsecured mobile homes, lawn furniture, toys.	4-5 feet
2	96-110	**Moderate:** mobile homes affected, rooftops damaged, flooding.	6-8 feet
3	111-130	**Extensive:** small buildings affected, low-lying roads flooded, electrical wires and trees down.	9-12 feet
4	131-155	**Extreme:** rooftops destroyed, trees and electrical wires down, mobile homes overturned, homes flooded etc.	13-18 feet
5	156+	**Catastrophic:** most buildings and vegetation destroyed, main roads flooded, homes flooded.	18+ feet

Knowing your Safety Risks

You can help reduce your safety risks when there is a pending storm by answering these questions.

1. Do your family live in a flood zone area? If so, what is your evacuation routes?

2. Do you have a family evacuation plan in place?

3. Is there a warning system in your area?

4. Have you packed a survival go-bag for each family member and your pets?

5. Is your home secured? Examples include:

    a. Clearing your yard of items that may blow away such as toys, plants, etc.

    b. Doors and windows covered with plyboards or window shutters.

Don't wait until the storm happens to figure it out.

PREPARE Today!

HURRICANE ALERTS

There are 2 types of hurricane alerts. Know the difference and what to do.

ALERT 1 – Hurricane Watch

If there is a '**Hurricane Watch**', this means there is a disturbance in the ocean possibly headed your way. When this happens you and your family should:

Start Preparing your Family and Home.

It includes:

- Staying informed by listening to your radio or local news.
- Boarding up windows at your home.
- Preparing survival go-bag(s)for all family members, including your pet(s).
- Knowing evacuation safe routes.

Be prepared to evacuate or shelter-in-place if directed to do so.

HURRICANE ALERTS (con'td)

ALERT 2 – Hurricane Warning

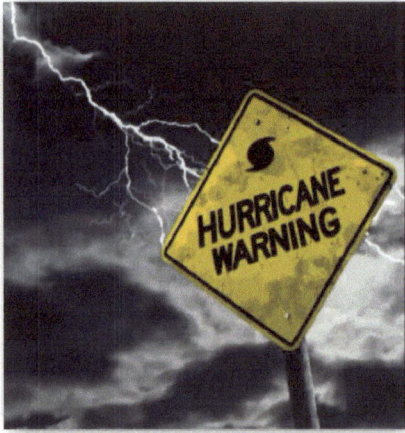

If you receive a **Hurricane Warning**, it means a disturbance in the ocean is approaching your area soon.
You and your family should:

Prepare to evacuate or shelter-in-place if directed.

- Have family and pet evacuation (go-bags) ready and available.
- Car filled with gas.
- Immediately following directions, do not hesitate.

REMEMBER: never stay or shelter-in-place in a mobile home as they are not safe.

Preparing in Advance:

The next steps is essential for your family to be safe when faced with a hurricane crisis.

STEP 1: Family Evacuation plan

- **CREATE** - a family evacuation plan that includes your pets.
- **PRACTICE** - your family evacuation plan at least 2 times a year.
- **TAKE ACTION** – by being ready to evacuate or shelter-in-place.
- Place your family evacuation plan where it can be reached when needed.
- Local officials will issue evacuations order based on flood zones.

STEP 2: Preparing your home

- Secured your home by boarding up all windows, patio doors, etc.
- Remove or secure any outdoor items that may fall or blow away due to high winds.

STEP 3: Survival Go-bags

A survival go-bag is a portable bag (or pillowcase) containing essential items that comes in handy in case of an evacuation. It's a great idea to have a survival go-bag ready for every family member, including your furry friends! This way, each of you has what you need to be comfortable for at least three days.

Survival Go-Bag for Kids

Kids survival go-bags should include items according to your age and needs.

These items can help you stay calm during stressful situations.

Essential Supplies

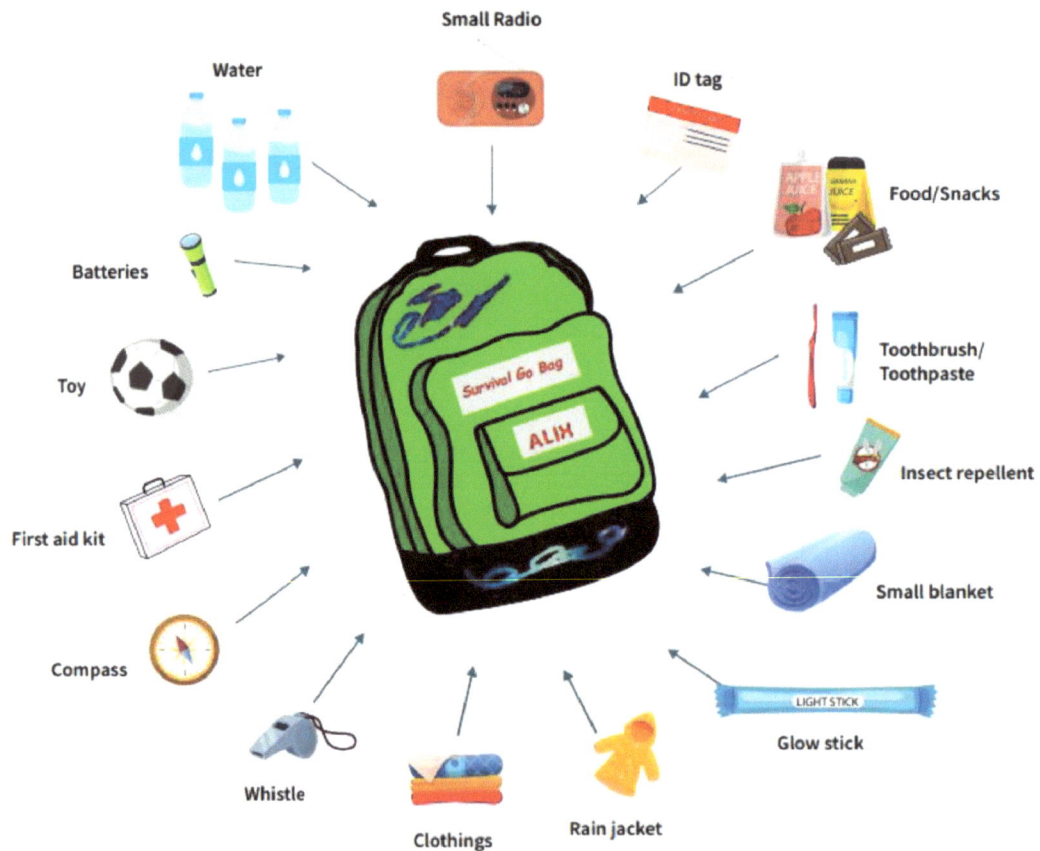

Survival Go-Bag for Pets:

Pets are a beloved part of the family; they rely on you to keep them safe. Be sure to include them in your evacuation plan and prepare a survival go-bag for them too!

Helpful tips in case of an evacuation:

a. Microchip your pets for their safety.

b. Coordinate with neighbors to care for or evacuate your pets if needed.

c. Find a safe drop-off location, as many hotels and shelters may not allow pets.

d. Contact your local animal control offices for more information and assistance, if needed.

Survival Go-Bag for Pets (cont'd):

Hey Family... don't forget about us!

We need supplies for 3 days

Water

PET FOOD DRY

Miss Sally

Mr. Logan

Pet Go-Bag
Sally

PET ID CARD
Place Pet Photo Here
Name
Breed
Chipped (yes/no)
Color
Owner
Contact
Medical Alert (if any)

REMEMBER: If it's not safe for you to stay behind, it's certainly not safe for a pet to be left behind.

Hurricane Safety Measures

- If sheltering -in-place, stay inside away from glass.
- Use only flashlights or glow sticks. **Never** use candles.
- Listen to the radio (battery operated) and follow evacuation orders provided by local officials and weather advisors.
- Avoid contact with floodwater, it may be contaminated with sewage, insects or other things living or dead.

Turn around ... Don't drown

Photograph: Emily Allen

REMEMBER: Moving water can cause a car to sink quickly.

AFTER A HURRICANE

After a hurricane, there are many dangerous elements that still remain, such as:

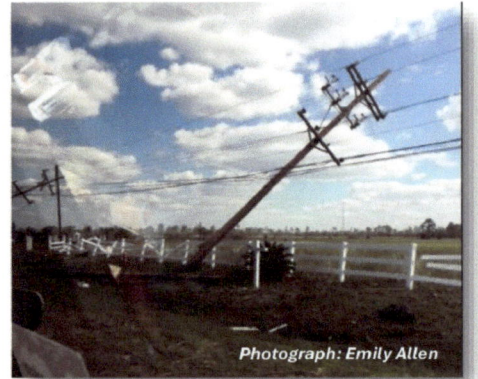

Photograph: Emily Allen

- Contaminated flood water

- Damaged building structures

- Fallen wires

- Uprooted and fallen trees

Important things to remember:

- Contact other family members and let them know you are safe.

- Continue to listen to local news to stay up-to-date on flooded areas, road closures, or when you can return to your home area.

- Do not play or wade in flooded areas as it may contain powerlines that are still active and contaminants such as raw sewage and other items filled with bacteria that can make you sick.

HURRICANE SAFETY REVIEW

1. Do you know if you live in a flood zone?

2. Do you have an evacuation plan?

3. Have you prepared your home?

4. Do you know the meaning of a storm 'Watch'?

5. Do you know the meaning a storm 'Warning'?

6. Do you have a survival go-bag prepared for each family member to last for at least 3 days?

7. Are your personal identification in a safe place where it can be collected immediately?

8. Are your pets included in your emergency evacuation plan?

9. Are your pets micro-chipped?

10. Are you prepared to shelter-in-place if needed?

NOTE: If you answered 'Yes' to all questions, you are awesome and ready! If not, please consider updating your action plan.

Certificate

Of

Awesomeness

In

"Hurricane Safety Measures"

Awarded to:

SuperHero

_____

For:

Being dedicated to safety and understanding my role in helping to
keep my family safe before, during and after a Hurricane.

_____

Date

~~UN~~PREPARED, LLC

REFLECTIONS:

Damage left by Hurricanes

Photographs by: Emily Allen

REFLECTIONS (cont'd):

Damage left by Hurricanes

Photographs by: Emily Allen

HURRICANE SAFETY CHECKLIST

❑   There is a family disaster plan in place.

❑   My family know of at least 2 travel routes in case of an evacuation.

❑   There are survival go-bags prepared for me, my family and pet(s) to maintain ourselves for at least 3 days.

❑   I live in a flood / non-flood zone area. *(circle one)*

❑   At least one of my family members are trained in First Aid.

❑   Car(s) filled with gas.

❑   My area has warning systems.

❑   Do you have personal credentials in a place where they can be accessed immediately?

SUMMARY

Don't wait until a disaster happens!

Preparing helps us to stay safe and recover quickly.

Are You and Your Family Prepared?

Be prepared to take action.

Other Volume(s)

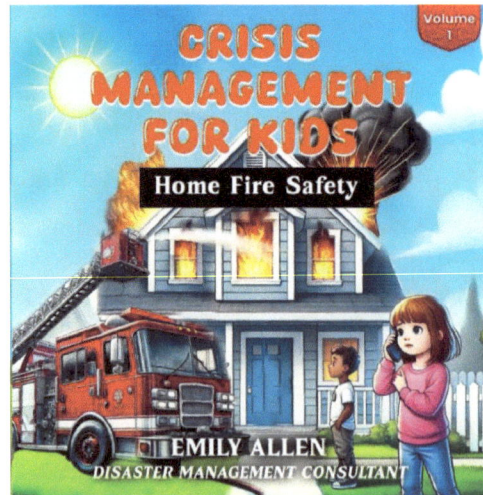

Amazon

www.ingramcontent.com/pod-product-compliance
Lightning Source LLC
LaVergne TN
LVHW072101070426
835508LV00002B/217